THE TOWER
OF LONDON
An artist's portrait

Annu Slit.

The White Tower

Hugh Casson

THE TOWER OF LONDON
An artist's portrait

with additional text (*An Historian's Viewpoint*)
by Richard White

The Herbert Press
in association with HM Tower of London

First published in Great Britain 1993 by
The Herbert Press Ltd, 46 Northchurch Road,
London N1 4EJ

House editor: Julia MacKenzie
Designed by Pauline Harrison

Set in Helvetica and Palatino by Selwood Systems,
Midsomer Norton.
Printed and bound in Great Britain by Butler & Tanner Ltd,
Frome, Somerset.

A CIP catalogue record for this book is available from the
British Library.

ISBN 1–871569–45–1

Introduction

The Tower of London – stone and brick, timber and iron – is a Castle on the Ground. No question. But there is also a touch of the nursery about it. The gilded cupolas and snapping flags, the white stone embroidery that gives a pretty edge to the rough texture of the walls, the oddly shaped toys that lie about on the turf-carpeted floor, elaborate cannon, prickly gates, window boxes, painted sentry boxes, little notices saying 'No milk today', huge rusting rings that once held fast a royal barge or an abandoned horse … and, casually positioned around all this, the Yeoman Warders dressed like brightly coloured dolls. All this seems to transform this Castle on the Ground at times into a Castle in the Air – whimsical, unexpected and engaging – in which the battlements and the calculated 'lines of fire' and bastions carefully planned by military engineers seem almost an irrelevance. As here indeed they proved to be. (The Tower of London was never involved in any battle except the occasional citizens' riot.) But all medieval castles, as we know, were homes as well as fortresses. They symbolized widely-spread powers, political as well as military, and their owners rode from one to the other like a chairman of industry visiting his network of factories. This mixture of solidity and permanence, of thick stone walls and temporarily imported comforts, sharpens the sense of theatre created by these multipurpose structures, reducing their menace and reminding us with their occasional gaiety – like a flowerpot on the window sill of a prison cell – that human life is still lived behind the battlements.

Just as extraordinary, if seldom recognized, is the fact that the Tower of London is also a triumph of design. How to reconcile successfully within a single complex the clutter of antagonistic functions and shapes and colours and materials into an harmonious visual pattern without imposing stylistic masks? It is done here by the English tradition of using diversity instead of imposing uniformity. The Tower in fact is a microcosm of the London that surrounds it. Unlike Paris or Vienna,

London is a city of secret places, of narrow alleyways, tiny squares and architectural surprises. No great boulevards, no endless avenues, no imposing 'rond-points'. In London as in the Tower, everybody feels there is something interesting just round the corner … And so there is.

Each building speaks the language of its time with confidence and often with wit, but without opening the dressing-up box. Changes of level are welcomed and encouraged to create visual interest; steps mount gently or dive suddenly downwards; people appear on the skyline or pass beneath the feet. Paving layouts delineate territory, sometimes changing texture to mark different areas of use. The original concept, built according to the laws of defence, remains clean and visually unchallenged, but everywhere tiny details are preserved and cared for – a mason's mark, a stone gulley, a heavy studded door, scratched initials on plaster and stone. All is linked by grass and trees. The traffic murmurs outside the walls and a smell of spices drifts across from the warehouses of Southwark, keeping all the senses busy and alert. There is nothing cute in sight. The whole place is a masterpiece of English urban landscape which is a pleasure to behold and to explore.

Author's Note

The order of the illustrations follows the recommended route round the Tower: through the Byward Tower, beneath the Bloody Tower up to Tower Green and St Peter ad Vincula, then the Waterloo Block and Crown Jewels, the White Tower and back to the river and the high-level wall-walk. Apart from a few restricted areas, visitors are free to wander as they please within the Tower walls. For the location of individual buildings see the map on pp. 62–3.

I am grateful to Richard White for contributing his text, 'An Historian's Viewpoint', and to Pamela Robinson for drawing the map.

5

the West Wall and Entrance Towers.

Nineteen towers regularly punctuate the curtain walls, like candles round the cake of the White Tower. They vary in size, use and interior grandeur, but from the outside they all look much the same – unsurprisingly since most were conscientiously restored or rebuilt during the nineteenth century. The accommodation was pretty standard: a lower chamber, often vaulted, planned originally for defence, but later used for storage and low-grade prisoners, and a first-floor apartment, with a fireplace and privy, for a distinguished victim or a Tower official. There are arrow-slit windows on the ground floor, lancet casements or sash windows higher up. Nearly all of them

carry on their interior wall a palimpsest of scratched initials or inscriptions, poignant or meaningless, made over the years either by prisoners or by bored and idle guards. Some of these are exquisitely elegant but it is sad to be told that they are probably the work of professionals hired to do them by the richer prisoners.

The 'stars' of these 'candles' are the entrance group – Middle, Byward and Bell towers – and the riverside group – St Thomas's, Bloody and Wakefield towers – and further north the Beauchamp and Martin towers.

Middle Tower.

The Middle and Byward towers (the present main entrance) contain
interesting interiors, fireplaces and square-topped windows. They
were each equipped with a double portcullis to guard the new
enlarged moat and a small private postern for the grandest visitors.

The Masters of the King's Works

In the Tower you are knowingly and unknowingly enveloped in manifestations of ideas and desires of long-dead wielders of royal power. Stand in Water Lane: imagine it is water, look up at the high wall by the Bell Tower. You are looking at three-quarters of a millennium of the work of severely practical and technically skilled men, architects, who carried out the bidding of royal clients: these were the Masters of the King's Works.

It is customary to refer to this tower or that wall as having been built by King X or Queen Y. This is not, of course, taken by anyone to mean that the monarch concerned personally laid stone on stone, or tottered up a ladder shouldering a hod of bricks. In fact, the degree of involvement or even interest shown by the monarch in works being engineered in their name varied widely.

All of this came to be administered by the office of the Clerk of Works. A visitor to this office, John Dawson, in 1472 describes having seen 'lying upon a counter ... a writing in paper ... containing the will and mind of King Henry VI in the devising of his sepulture'. The unfortunate Henry VI had been murdered, tradition has it, while at prayers in the Wakefield Tower on 21 May 1471, but had obviously expressed his desires to his architect on the form of his tomb.

The great blocks of Sussex marble which form much of the Bell Tower and some of the wall running from it towards the Bloody Tower along Water Lane, once washed by the Thames, were laid for Richard I in swaggering Plantagenet style. The works, on the King's

authority, were entrusted by his chancellor, William Longchamp, to his brother, Osbert, keeper of the king's houses, who in turn delegated direct supervision to Roger Enganet – the 'engineer'. (The term 'ingeniator' is used in medieval records to express the profession of architect, aptly enough for there is, after all, much ingenuity and engineering in good building.) Therefore, the grace within and the controlled force without the Bell Tower are no monument to Richard the Lionheart. Far from it, for this paradoxically warmly-remembered King of England spent barely six months of his eleven-year reign in this country; pressed for cash, he is alleged to have said, 'I would sell London if I could find a buyer.' Neither should the Longchamp brothers be given much credit. The Bell Tower is a monument to the ingenious Roger and the skill of the masons he directed eight hundred years ago.

In 1190 £2881 1s. 10d. were spent on the works within the Tower – a staggering sum, every silver penny of which had to be accounted for.

Records of financial transactions made by the Exchequer were kept on sheets of vellum which were sewn together to form a continuous strip for each financial year. These strips were kept rolled up, like wallpaper, and from early days were nicknamed 'pipe-rolls'. They and other enrolled accounts are of immeasurable importance in unravelling what officially happened and when, but then as now there is a certain flexibility between the official record and what was actually done.

Bell Tower from the Wharf.

The Bell Tower (attached to Queen's House) is the oldest of all the
towers with walls ten-feet thick and nearly sixty-feet high. The belfry
itself is a chirpy seventeenth-century addition. Distinguished
prisoners included Sir Thomas More and Princess Elizabeth.

Most sophisticated of all is St Thomas's Tower on the reclaimed river shore and guarding what is now known as Traitors' Gate. Here were the royal sleeping quarters attached to the Wakefield Tower's reception rooms by a connecting, now rebuilt, bridge. Stained glass and sculpture were featured externally.

Traitors' Gate

In the mid thirteenth century, for example, the barons of the Exchequer were dismayed to discover that the sheriffs of the City of London had asked for reimbursement of £30 remitted to the keeper of the works at the Tower 'before they had paid one penny'. The king, Henry III, was furious at the 'great harm' suffered in entrusting works to sheriffs and other officers and on 29 November 1256 ordered that in future, Master John, the king's mason, and Master Alexander, the king's carpenter, should see that the works were performed on a day-work or fixed-price basis. Master John died in the summer of 1260 and was succeeded by Master Robert of Beverley, who ranks as one of the greatest masters of thirteenth-century military architecture. He, more than any other individual, was responsible for making the vast concentric fortress, begun by Henry III and completed by his son, Edward I, a physical reality.

In 1378 there was another shake-up resulting in the appointment of John Blake as Clerk of the (King's) Works and on the same day William Hanney as Comptroller, thus beginning an unbroken four centuries of holders of these posts with an office in Westminster where Cromwell's statue now stands. The Clerks were by no means simple book-keepers, but were for the most part competent and literate administrators, expected to travel widely in overseeing the works. Geoffrey Chaucer was Clerk from 1389 to 1391 with a grant of £20 a year from Richard II. He was not paid anything until 1394 so it is perhaps as well he had a sideline. It was, one suspects, the authentic voice of real experience which caused him to write: 'And therefore, at the kynge's court, my brother, Ech man for hymselfe, ther is noon other' (*Canterbury Tales*, The Knight's Tale, 1, 1181).

On his visit to the Office of Works in 1472, John Dawson did not only see Henry VI's prescient ideas for his tomb, but also 'portraying tables of wainscot' and 'panels of Estrich [wood from Norway or the Baltic] boards made in order to draw out divers towers theron'. Alas, not one of the plans drawn on these boards has survived from the Middle Ages, but the accounts are in pretty good shape. In the world of the Masters of the King's Works, in other words, the paymaster not only called the tune, but also took the credit.

The Clerk kept detailed inventories of stock – from cranes and pile-drivers ('falling rammes') to the least of innumerable types of nails simply called 'trassh'. Mention is also made of the Master Mason's 'long oak chest made to keep the patrons and instruments' with which he practised his craft. In medieval times the construction of the building and its detailed design proceeded together, following templates ('patrons') for details of mouldings and the like, and using a set of geometrical formulae from which the three-dimensional structure could be developed on site from a small-scale plan without an intermediate design stage requiring the production of hundreds of detailed drawings. The medieval master mason employed 'tricks of the trade' which formed a secret lore, jealously guarded, like that of early navigators or astronomers. The freemasons developed a system of secret signs for mutual recognition and an obligation to help brother masons in times of need. Each would have his own mark – a rune-like carving – from which work could be recognized and paid for accordingly.

So, paradoxically, it came to be that the vast palace and fortress of the Tower of London, so much the outward statement of the authority of the Crown and of the nationhood of England, was built in conditions of closely-maintained secrecy among the master-craftsmen who were its first architects.

Bloody Tower
Sir Walter Raleigh's Bedroom.

The Bloody Tower (once the Garden Tower) is built over the older watergate – the mooring rings for boats still survive. It boasted two portcullises – one remains – and contained well-appointed apartments. Sir Walter Ralegh spent thirteen years in this tower writing his *History of the World* (he got as far as the Roman Empire before his execution) and Judge Jeffreys died here of drink.

The Mooring Ring

Queen's House.

This timber-framed building occupies the southwest corner of the Tower enclosure and is the official residence of the Governor. Today, Queen's House, not open to visitors, is a comfortable-looking collection of apartments; offices huddle cosily on the ground floor;

Queen's House
Anne Boleyn's
Bedroom

a busy domestic life is enjoyed in the two upper floors where four-poster beds and Tudor panelling adorn the spare rooms reputedly once occupied by distinguished prisoners – Lady Jane Grey, Anne Boleyn, Katherine Howard and last of all, in 1941, Rudolf Hess, who briefly stayed in the west wing. But the cheerful chintz and wide windows do not quite succeed in dispelling the memory of the previous unhappy occupants.

Lower Bell Tower.
Sir Thomas More's Cell.

The grandest room is the still-used Council Chamber on the first floor. Beneath the lofty timbered ceiling the chairs meet silently round the carved table. On the wall a richly coloured and inscribed marble panel records the examination in this room of Guy Fawkes. After being put on the rack he returned to this room to be sentenced to be hanged, drawn and quartered.

Queen's House.
The Council Chamber

An Historian's Viewpoint

'Fear Death by Water'

Sir Walter Ralegh spent much of his fifteen years or so as a prisoner in the Tower in the Bloody Tower in some comfort, among other activities brewing up his home-made hooch and carrying out more-or-less scientific experiments of a chemical nature in a converted chicken shed in the adjacent garden now known as Tower Green. This popular adventurer went to the block in Westminster Palace Yard on 29 October 1618.

Being 'sent to the Tower' is an expression which conjures up images of a fate which might well include death. The taking of a human life is not only the worst of crimes, it is a mortal sin and the men of the Middle Ages felt this just as strongly as we do. Popular mythology has the stone chambers of the Tower drenched in blood but in fact the vast majority of Lieutenants and Yeoman Warders of the Tower viewed their occasional role as gaolers and inquisitors with distaste and more than once lent assistance or turned a blind eye to the escape of prisoners.

Bishop Latimer, who had been imprisoned in the Tower once before, was held there again on his way to be burned at the stake at Oxford in October 1555. He gives a glimpse, not only of his bravery, but also the relationship many prisoners developed with the warders: 'What, my old friend,' he said to one, 'how do you? I am now come to be your neighbour again.'

Ralegh, to his misfortune, suffered under the unsympathetic regime of a Lieutenant whom he characterized as 'that beast Waad'. Such men were rarities.

It is the bloody spasm of political and religious conflict in the Tudor period which is largely responsible for the evil reputation of the Tower. The wielders of power did nothing to disenchant people of this, for the threat of the possibility of violence can often be as

Queen's House.

effective as violence itself. Few would not confess all or anything when faced with the threat of a white-hot iron rod or a hammer, never mind the rack.

There were no specially constructed dungeons or torture-chambers within the Tower, but from time to time most of the older buildings were pressed into service as places of confinement. One such was the upper chamber of the Bell Tower, where the Catholic Queen Mary imprisoned her half-sister, Anne Boleyn's daughter, Elizabeth for a short time in 1554.

Princess Elizabeth arrived by water, through Traitors' Gate beneath St Thomas's Tower on a dismal Palm Sunday in teeming rain. She was twenty years old and fearful of the place which she had described as 'more wonted for a false traitor than a true subject'. The cloak proffered by the Lord Treasurer was declined with a touch of her hand. Alighting into the water lapping the steps of Traitors' Gate she paused to address the group formed up to receive her, including the Constable, Sir John Gage, warders and officers: 'Here landeth as true a subject being a prisoner, as ever landed at these steps.'

This young woman, destined to give her name to a golden age of English history, was held behind locked doors in fear of her life. She was allowed to take exercise along the short length of wall-walk linking the upper Bell Tower to the Beauchamp. It is still known as 'Princess Elizabeth's Walk'. Later, Elizabeth was to stay here as queen for two days but, having left for her coronation, she never returned, seeming, with no little justification, to have hated the place. She hardly bothered with it, never even appointing a Constable – a gap in an otherwise unbroken chain of holders of that office to the present day. And you will search the Tower in vain for that busy, glassy grace which marks the best of Elizabethan architecture.

Queens' House
Princess Elizabeth's walk.

20 Beauchamp Tower.
    Tower Green

The Beauchamp Tower replaced the ruined landgate from the City (see p.22) and it was usually reserved for prisoners of rank. There is plenty of medieval brickwork visible and a wealth of inscriptions. Look for the Dudley memorial recording the imprisonment in 1533 of John Dudley, Duke of Northumberland, for plotting to place Lady Jane Grey on the throne. A large fireplace and a generous nineteenth-century window dominate the first-floor apartment.

We must be careful before we regret this too much and remember that four hundred years ago the Tower was regarded as damp, old-fashioned and unfit for the Elizabethan court, even without the Queen's unpleasant memories. Had it been decided to bring the palace up-to-date much would have been demolished to make way for the streaming light and optimism of that age. This is not to say that the Tower would have been spoiled or debased; it would have been different. Such are the accidents of history.

Antiquity, of course, does not necessarily imbue buildings with structural quality, although that which has been poorly-made or designed is less likely to have survived to be a problem to the conservation architect of today. Jerry-building, in other words, is not confined to our own age.

The Tower was not exempt from it either, for a newly-built gatehouse on the site of the

present Beauchamp Tower collapsed catastrophically on 23 April 1240 (St George's Day). In this case St Thomas à Becket got the blame, his ghost having been seen banging the rubble with his crozier, intoning 'You will never build here'. Why his ghost, albeit of a

former Constable of the Tower, took exception to the gatehouse is not recorded.

The architect was lucky to have had a ghost to blame. In fact he had built the gatehouse over a recently filled-in moat and had failed to allow for the softer ground when specifying the foundations. Archeological excavation has shown the massive size of the foundations of the Beauchamp, which was built for Edward I in 1281 to replace the failed gatehouse.

By the reign of Elizabeth the Tower had totally changed within the high-tech walls of Edward I's killing-machine. It clanked and chattered with industry: clerical, mechanical and military, but its days of use as a royal palace were over.

School Picnic

Town Green near the Execution site.

Outside St Peter ad Vincula, the tiny black execution block with its list of victims rules its grassy kingdom with ease and modesty. (When in use it was placed upon a high scaffold for the delight of onlookers.) Scholars may dismiss it as a tourist gimmick but voices noticeably become quieter as visitors approach the spot – and no wonder, for the courage and dignity of the victims brings tears to the eyes: Anne Boleyn, who asked to be beheaded not by the axe but by the sword: 'Pray for the King,' she said, 'for he is a good man … and I die willingly'; Katherine Howard, who asked for the block to be brought to her cell so she could practise laying her head upon it: 'I die a Queen, but I would rather die the wife of Culpeper'; the sixteen-year-old Lady Jane Grey who publicly accepted the justice of her sentence.

St Peter ad Vincula.
The Tomb of John Holland.
Duke of Exeter.

St Peter ad Vincula
The Blount Memorial

The houses crawl to a final halt as they reach St Peter ad Vincula – a pretty Tudor building replacing the original medieval local parish church (see p. 47). Within are really spectacular tombs – the Duke of Exeter and his three wives, their yellowing faces smoothly engraved; Richard Cholmondly and his wife, rich and confident; some splendid wall tablets. Underfoot lie about 1,500 headless victims of the axe, including three queens who were executed on the block which can be seen through the windows. The royal corpses were later exhumed by order of Queen Victoria and reburied with proper decorum. Don't miss the small chapel dedicated to Sir Thomas More which has been carved out of the crypt. The church itself is friendly and full of light but the solemn faces of the recumbent effigies and the thought of what lay or still lies beneath the paving is dispiriting.

Tomb of the Master of the Ordnance

St Peter ad Vincula

Waterloo Block
St Peter ad Vincula.

A notice near the Waterloo Block invites the visitor to 'Toilets, Torture Instruments, Education Centre'. It is the torture instruments, needless to say, which seem to attract the longest queues.

Standing to attention alongside the north wall is the Waterloo Block itself – built as barracks on the orders of the Duke of Wellington to house 1,000 men. It wears its uniform with a light touch. It carries the obligatory parapet of stage battlements, and the windows are not pretend arrow slits but generous and lofty.

The sign read.....

Toilets
Torture Instruments
Education Centre

Until recently, most of this impressive building was devoted to an exhibition of oriental armour, including the wonderful elephant armour captured in India. The live military is now confined to a couple of upper floors … an office, a dormitory, a canteen and an officer's flat. It is dead quiet. Off-duty soldiers doze on their beds. The cruets stand as if 'on duty' on the tables. There is a faint smell of boot polish and gravy.

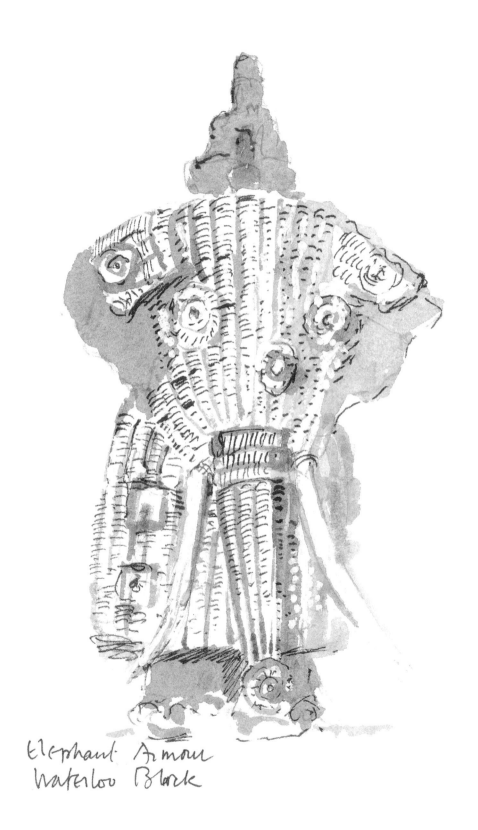

Elephant Armour
Waterloo Block

Waterloo Block — an exploded view.

32

Castles in the Air

Castles are supposed to be ruins, replete with ivy and wallflowers, perhaps the odd archeological dig and a custodian who knows all about the place. The Tower has all of these and more. A couple of hundred years ago it had a stinking moat, a menagerie and several pubs, with attendant pickpockets and whores. Earlier, as we have seen, it housed the court with all the dignity of an ancient monarchy. It is a place of constant change but singular purpose – to be the Royal Palace and Fortress of the monarch of the United Kingdom. The Crown Jewels are held here under vigilant guard. They are the real thing, no matter which gossip tells you to the contrary.

There is a dynamic conservatism about the place. The imperatives of preservation and conservation vie with the pressures of tourism and economics. One supposes it has never been an easy place to run and one need not envy the task of the Resident Governor in striving to reconcile what must often be conflicting interests or points of view.

The soldiers who sleep or remain unblinkingly on guard here may neither dream nor think of the remorseless clockwork of governance which has been exercised from here, but their heartbeats are just as much a part of the place as the cobbles or the White Tower itself.

Sleeping soldier.
Waterloo "Barracks."

In the basement of the Waterloo Block (until they are moved upstairs) are the peripatetic Crown Jewels. Most of them are seventeenth century, made to replace those destroyed by the Parliamentarians or damaged later by fire. Huge steel doors and armoured glass guard a sudden explosion of gold and silver, of coloured velvets, multi-flashing jewels and gems, sceptres, dishes, spurs, crowns and medals. This almost terrifying display of temporal wealth and symbolic power, despite its dazzle and delicate intricacy, somehow lowers the spirits, and the visitors shuffling round, half-blinded and half-shocked by the sparkling glare, are reduced to whispering in the presence of so much conspicuous display.

School Party.
Hospital Block and New Armouries

Hospital Brooke

the New Armouries.
1664.

To the east of the White Tower stands a group of three formal but friendly post-medieval buildings. The first, once the Tower officers' mess, contains the very well-presented Fusiliers Regimental Museum. The second (once a hospital) now provides accommodation for Tower officials, while the third contains, grasped within its fine seventeenth-century timber framework, the offices of the Royal Armouries and some of their displays.

All three buildings are handsome but somehow look like uninvited guests, their backs against the perimeter wall, waiting to be spoken to.

New Armouries
Sculptured
Coat of Arms

Facing onto the White Tower, on their once-cobbled carpet of turf, stand the post-medieval rosy-faced official houses. Their blue front doors and white sash windows stare with dignified courtesy across what looks like a college quad or cathedral close … an impression strengthened by the Tower ravens lurching and hobbling across the grass, flapping their black wings like gowns and cassocks as if in some sort of Trollopian ballet. Beautiful, glossy, self-assured, these birds are often ill-tempered and don't mind adding to their official diet of cheese and horseflesh with a few nips from the hands of those attempting to feed them.

The White Tower
from The New Armouries

The White Tower (for centuries it was whitewashed), the oldest Norman keep in England, was the true power-centre of the Tower of London and beneath its coronet of cupolas it looks it. Foursquare (except for its southwest corner), it was built as the donjon. Behind its façade of yellowish-grey ragstone embroidered with Portland and Caen stone lie the royal apartments on the first and second floors, marked outside by their huge arched windows. It has suffered numerous facelifts over the centuries, but the entrance is still at the original first-floor level, and circular staircases continue to occupy the corner turrets. There is a well in the basement, two fireplaces and two latrines on the first floor, and one fireplace and three latrines on the second floor. Behind the fifteen-foot-thick walls are impressive floor spaces and heavily beamed ceilings that today brood darkly over the ranks of silent, armoured figures.

Henry III's Wall
and Ravens' Huts.

At present, the White Tower contains a three-floored exhibition of weapons and armour – for men and horses, for battle or beflagged tournaments. The figures, a mixture of the comic and the sinister, stoop slightly towards the visitor, their arms hanging helplessly like Hollywood spacemen. They are polished and brightly lit, their surfaces undented by rust or scars, their joints ingeniously detailed and prettily engraved. Ladies hoping for a child would prick with a pin a giant metal codpiece forming part of Henry VIII's suit of armour. (The practice was later forbidden by the Church.) Every room seems more like an ogre's 'batterie de cuisine' designed for display rather than for active use. For those who enjoy this impressive military parade, and wish to study its ingenuity and decorative detail, here on show is surely one of the finest collections in the world. No craftsman's skill of this quality can fail to be interesting and often beautiful, but to those (like myself) whose heart does not leap in these quiet and threatening rooms, the words that spring to mind are heavy with tragedy – courage, pain, fear, exaltation, futility, defeat and death – and I am always glad to escape.

Picnic.

The area around and below the tower once hummed and buzzed with noise and activity – visitors, workmen, armourers and servants constantly at work. The Mint, separately staffed for security, thrived, as did the menagerie. Lions lived in handsome arcades and an elephant presided. A popular animal was a polar bear, who fished his lunch for himself with his paw from the river Thames.

Embedded in this fairytale collection is St John's, one of the most beautiful little Norman churches in Europe, once a record-store; a tiny masterpiece of simplicity. The vaulted aisles march sedately round the semi-domed apse; the nave is barrel-vaulted. The capitals of the columns are strongly carved. Windows as clear as a glass of water – no gilded frippery – built of faintly textured stone from which the original plaster and paint work have long-since gone. It reeks of conviction, a simple statement of faith so moving that it never fails to call the crowd of visitors to silence.

The White Tower
Basement Display.

White Tower
Chapel of St John the Evangelist

45

Arrow Slit. Water Lane.

Children stand where the river once ran. A brightly-lighted arrow slit
shines out from the sooty emplacement.

God and Mammon

The outer bailey of the Tower, between the inner and outer walls, is known as Mint Street. Coins were struck in workshops ranged along it from at least the late thirteenth century until August 1812 when the move to new workshops on Little Tower Hill was complete.

In 1546 the maker of melting-pots for the Tower Mint, William Foxley, fell asleep and slept for fourteen days and fifteen nights. On waking, 'as if he had slept but one', he continued at his labours until his death in 1587.

Turning an ingot of precious metal into a good coin calls for the highest exercise of artistry, ingenuity, craftsmanship and brute force that can be mustered. The overworked William Foxley was part of a major industrial enterprise which was crucial not only to the economic wellbeing of the realm, but also the authority and reputation of the monarch. The gold or silver had to be pure and the weight correct. For example, there had to be 240 pennies to the pound of silver, a way of counting money which remained in use in England from AD 100 until decimalization in 1971. Coiners, forgers or counterfeiters risked harsh punishment, even death, because causing a lack of trust in the worth of currency undermined confidence in the monarch. Until this century, coins were generally of gold or silver, especially the latter, and the practice of clipping or shaving the edges of coins was a common but dangerous way of, in effect, stealing from the Crown. Sir Lewis Stukeley betrayed his kinsman, Sir Walter Ralegh, to James I and was paid the handsome sum of £965 6s. 3d. for this unpopular act of treachery. As it happened, he was caught clipping the very coins he (now nicknamed 'Sir Judas Stukeley') had been paid. 'Sir Judas' was duly taken to the Tower under sentence of death. James pardoned him but Stukeley, shunned by everyone, died a raving lunatic on Lundy Island barely two years later, in August 1620.

The words and letters running round the edge of the 'heads' side of British coinage contains, in abbreviated form, the name and titles of the monarch: ELIZABETH II D.G. REG. F.D., stands for 'Dei Gratia Regina Fidei Defensor' – 'by the grace of God, Queen, Defender of the Faith'. 'Fidei Defensor' is a title bestowed on Henry VIII by Pope Leo X in 1521 in recognition of a book written by Henry in defence of the Catholic church against attack by Martin Luther. In the political arena, conflict between Catholics and Protestants caused death and suffering to many, but Christian worship, Catholic or Protestant, has continued within the Tower from its very beginning to the present day.

The religious needs of the inhabitants of the Tower from king to kitchen-boy were catered for by two chapels and two oratories. As one might expect, the architectural history of these holy places reflects the changes made to the Tower as a whole, particularly the Chapel Royal of St Peter ad Vincula. There has been a church or chapel on this spot from at least the early twelfth century and quite probably earlier. The present chapel is a fine example of early Tudor work, built for Henry VIII in 1519–20 following a fire which virtually destroyed the chapel built for Edward I some 250 years earlier.

Within the White Tower lies the Chapel of St John the Evangelist, virtually unchanged since it was built under the direction of Gundulph, Bishop of Rochester in 1078. Almost every English monarch since the twelfth century has worshipped in this simple but soul-quietening place. Stout and tough-looking, like the king who ordered it to be made, the Chapel of St John ranks among the finest achievements of Norman architecture.

Yeoman Warders' Homes in the Casemates.

48

the Signpost.

Buried in the thickness of the curtain walls
are residences of the Yeoman Warders –
like mews cottages or tiny birds' nests,
their façades alive with window boxes.
Washing flaps gaily on the flat roofs and
cats doze on doorsteps, and children's
toys stare impassively out from the
casement windows.

As silent as houseflies a group of dolls stare at us from a casement window: watchful, and secure behind the polished glass from passing challenges. Despite their baby colours and softly knitted jackets they seem to carry a disconcerting message of authority and ownership, and passers-by seem uneasy in their presence.

The Well Tower

A typical corner of the Tower: a complex of periods, materials and uses, romantic, mysterious and as strong as stone; steps plunge down to narrow, almost sinister, little doors; a railing marks the presence of a higher-level walk. Medieval masonry is balanced with the Victorian restoration by Anthony Salvin. All gracefully united by some anonymous creative eye for the picturesque.

Tower Bridge

This is the best view in London of
Tower Bridge, a worthy architectural
companion to the Tower itself. Two
men share the design honours – the
City architect Sir Horace Jones, the
jolly, globular son of a solicitor, and
Sir John Wolfe–Barry, the railway
expert son of Sir Charles Barry,
architect of the Palace of Westminster.
The builder was Sir William Arrol,
head of the company responsible
for the Forth Bridge. The problem
here was to provide a bridge high
enough to permit the passage of
largish ships and at a place where
there was no room to provide
approach-road ramps. The solution –
half suspension, half drawbridge, all
dressed up in Gothic finery – is
masterly and rivals Big Ben as the
popular symbol of London.

Reached from the high-level wall-walk, the Martin Tower is a popular favourite among the parade of towers that march along the inner curtain wall. No wonder, for its appearance, devoid of nineteenth-century restorations, is as variegated and engaging as its history. Its attractions are immediate. Entrance is beneath a pretty, modern sundial and up a couple of narrow steps through a cupboard-sized door. Within awaits an interior of puzzling complexity: sash windows, a splendid fireplace, a staircase. Painted panelling partially conceals medieval stonework bearing initials and inscriptions. This was the attractive penthouse flat of the Keeper of the Jewel House – you could almost move in tomorrow if you didn't mind the ghost which was said by the Keeper of the time to resemble a glass tube filled with blueish fluid and which circled the dining table between courses.

On the floor below, now the home of the Torture Museum, once rested the Crown Jewels, where they were informally displayed and could by request be handled or even tried on by visitors. Not surprisingly they were stolen in 1671 by a well-spoken but impudent fellow called Captain Blood. Disguised as a clergyman and helped by a female accomplice who diverted attention by fainting, Blood made off, but was captured, pardoned (and for some reason pensioned) and the Jewels recovered.

Sir Christopher Wren renovated the tower and it subsequently survived the fire of 1841 (when nobody could find the keys), and the rescued Jewels fetched up in the Wakefield Tower until 1967.

The Martin Tower

An Historian's Viewpoint

Killing at a Distance

The Tower of London has been described as a
'village'. It has a small, closely-knit hierarchi-
cal resident population which lives in
and among buildings which date back almost
a thousand years. Typically English, there is a
pub, a church, a chapel, a bird-bath on the
green, a manor house and a castle. These days
the milkman delivers in his milk float and the
binmen take the rubbish away; children go off
to school; tourists arrive; people get married,
baptized, and die here. But it is not a village,
and has never been one. It was built as, and
remains, a physical expression of royal power,
real and remembered. Paradoxically, it is also
a manifestation of that insecurity which
anyone who locks a drawer or a door demon-
strates. In the Tower you are never far
from armaments, ancient and modern. It is a
place of high security: the Crown Jewels alone
justify a battalion and to this day the senior
serving military officer in the Tower (usually
a Colonel) is from the Ordnance Corps.

NO
MILK
TO DAY

Queen's House

This place was built with the ultimate
purpose of keeping safe what or whoever was
inside, and to keep those who might threaten
this security at the greatest distance possible.
It has never been called 'London Castle',
although it surely has the title deeds to be so
named. No, it is *arx palatina*, royal palace, and
whatever was kept or made or held within its
curtilage was and still is under royal protec-
tion. So we have the Royal Palace and
Fortress of the Tower of London, unique in the
continuity of its use as such and special in the
conditions imposed by its role to defend the
exercise of royal power from attack by a foe
more likely to come from the inhabitants of the
City of London than any invading power.

Technology and armaments are inseparably
intertwined, and the buildings, certainly those
of the high middle ages, are a response to

technological advance, like the Beauchamp
Tower, which was built to protect the
landward approach from the City of London.
This massive tower, equipped with all the
latest ways of killing people at a distance with
crossfire from crossbows, stood as a constant
reminder to the citizens of London of the final
military sanction available to their sovereign.

Just as William the Conqueror's White
Tower had been the peak of the military
technology of its age, each phase of the
development of the Tower as a military
structure closely follows the technology of the
age. Military necessity precluded any respect
for the antiquity or historical associations of
rooms or buildings; much was swept aside to
adapt the medieval buildings to take account
of an ever-increasing pace of technological
innovation.

Tower of London — Legge's Mount
N. W. corner.

Tower of London
N. E. corner.

This robust thirteenth-century bastion on the northwest corner of the outer curtain echoes its opposite fellow on the northeast angle. Both were designed as a firing platform and keep a masterful grip on the curtain wall – behind which the pinnacle towers and battlements of the Tower create their pretty silhouette. (A third, nineteenth-century bastion, positioned between the other two, was destroyed in a wartime air raid and not rebuilt.)

Hospital Block from the East

Flemish Cannon

Gunpowder made a huge difference; the ingeniously elaborate defensive structures of medieval castles were rendered anachronisms with the first firing of a cannon. The Tower is littered with cannon, many of them trophies of war, cold with the silent possibility of a violence far more distant and undiscriminating than that of the sword. Medieval towers were cut down and their lower chambers filled with the resulting rubble in order to provide solid platforms from which to try out these new weapons: the Tower was to become a ship on land.

Works put in hand in 1682 included

'The making of a large Platform of Oaken timber upon the Leads of St Thomas Tower over Traytors Gate marked upon the draught to the river side 80 foot long 30 foot broad Plancked with 3 inch Oaken Plancks being for 9 guns. This Platform is necessary to be done having a fflanck on each side for two Guns to cleare the Ditch or Graft will cost £294.'

The Tower, like any castle, had always been humming with ideas of violence, both invasive and defensive. The manufacture and storage of armaments made increasing demands on the usable space within the Tower from the reign of Henry VIII onwards –

'the armourie for warlike provision' as John Stow has it (1525–1605). Late sixteenth and early seventeenth-century inventories give a glimpse of the extent of the provision for the manufacture and maintenance of ordnance within the Tower. Apart from the long-established storehouses in Coldharbour there was the Pike House, Bill House, Arrow Lofte, Small Gun Office, Rich Weapon House, Inner and Outer Iron Houses and the Upper Ordnance House.

As Sarah Barter, Librarian of the Royal Armouries has written, 'The Restoration in fact marked the beginning of a period of rapid expansion both in the functions of the Office of Ordnance in the country and in its physical environment within the Tower.' The major remaining structural evidence of this initiative is the New Armouries, built with great dispatch in 1663–4 on, as the royal warrant described, 'that void and waste piece of ground within our said Tower commonly known [as] the Wardrobe Garden'.

The nineteenth century was to see another phase of conflict or perhaps more properly, debate, concerning the structure of the Tower. The Constable of the time, none other than the Duke of Wellington, instigated the building of the Waterloo Barracks to replace the Grand Storehouse destroyed in a disastrous fire in 1841, and wished to return the Tower to a purely military base. Meanwhile, the Prince Consort to Queen Victoria, Albert, had a wider vision and this resulted in a largely successful reconstruction of the Tower as a fortress-cum-tourist attraction under the direction of one of the premier architects of the day, Anthony Salvin.

The debate continues. Every change to either the fabric or way of life of the Tower is carefully considered and discussed before being implemented. The place hums with life and the keys to the Tower still unlock the gates of English history.

Sometimes grim but more often relaxed, even pretty at times, the Tower carries its complicated history in an assembly of architecture as casually mixed as the High Street of an old market town – turf and trees triumph over relics of despotism. Shoals of school children peer cheerfully over the battlements, cannon are aimed only upon the sparrows.

Terrible things, we know, have happened in this place but (as all of us remember from our schooldays) cruelty and injustice always take place against a background of the ordinary. Behind the crash of the axe or the loneliness of the pinnioned prisoner, birds continue to sing, leaves to fall. Bread is baked, songs are whistled, rainwater seeks the falling tide.

The Wharf.
West End.

the Tower of London
from the river   Byward Tower   Bell Tower   Queen's Hou
                    Queen's Stairs

White Tower   Lanthorn Tower

St Thomas' Tower
Traitors Gate

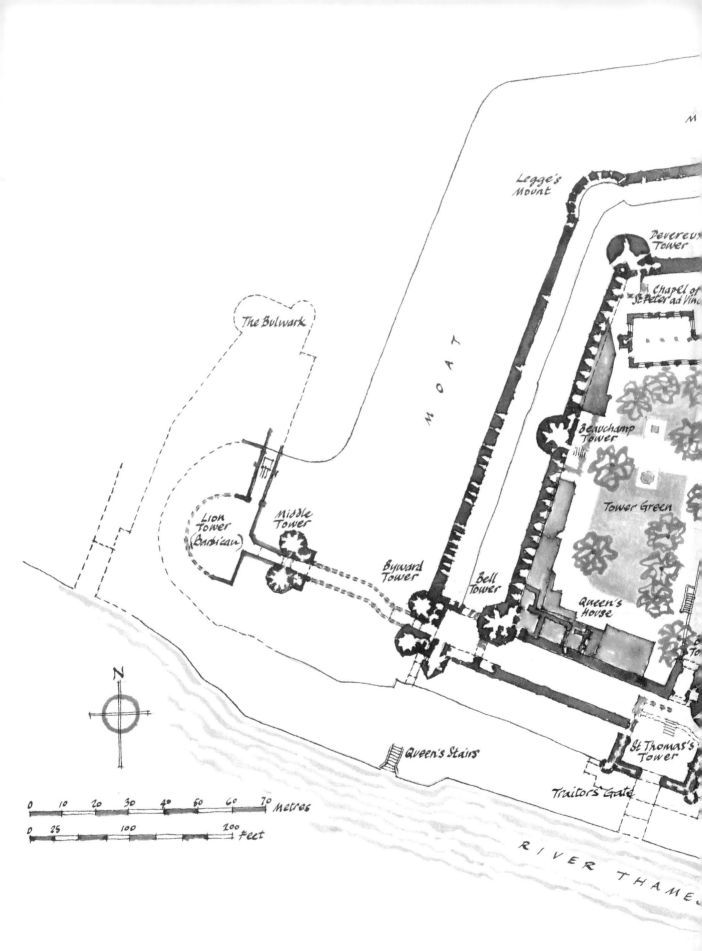

The Bulwark

MOAT

Legge's Mount

Devereux Tower

Chapel of St Peter ad Vin...

Beauchamp Tower

Tower Green

Lion Tower (Barbican)

Middle Tower

Byward Tower

Bell Tower

Queen's House

N

Queen's Stairs

St Thomas's Tower

Traitor's Gate

0 10 20 30 40 50 60 70 Metres

0 25   100   200 Feet

RIVER THAMES

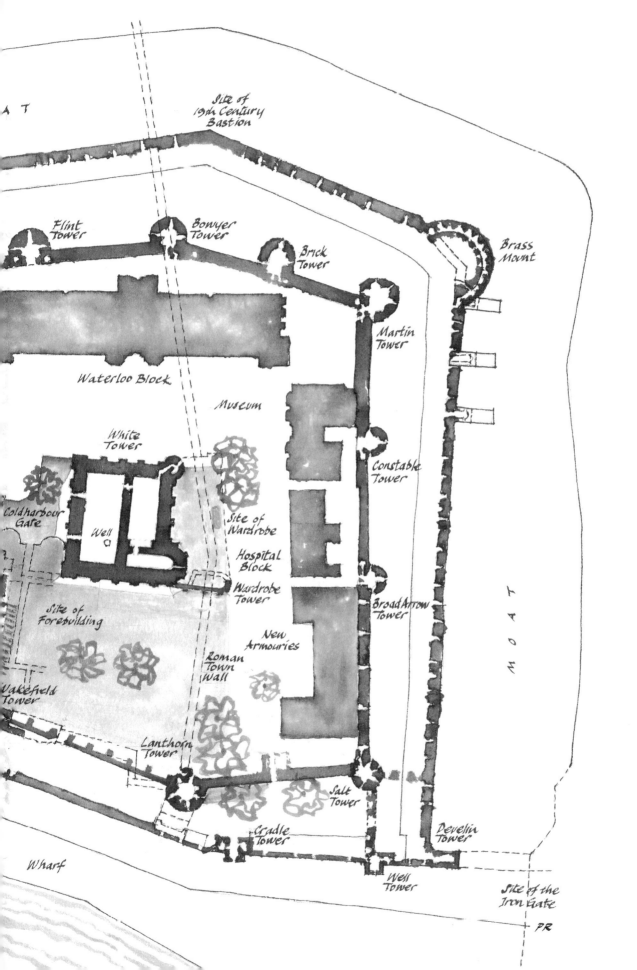

Site of
19th Century
Bastion

Flint
Tower

Bowyer
Tower

Brick
Tower

Brass
Mount

Martin
Tower

Waterloo Block

Museum

White
Tower

Constable
Tower

Coldharbour
Gate

Site of
Wardrobe

Well

Hospital
Block

Wardrobe
Tower

Site of
Forebuilding

Broad Arrow
Tower

New
Armouries

M O A T

Roman
Town
Wall

Wakefield
Tower

Lanthorn
Tower

Salt
Tower

Develin
Tower

Cradle
Tower

Wharf

Well
Tower

Site of the
Iron Gate

PR